The Escape

Or, A Leap for Freedom

WILLIAM WELLS BROWN

COSIMOCLASSICS

NEW YORK

The Escape Or, A Leap for Freedom
Cover © 2007 Cosimo, Inc.

For information, address:

Cosimo, P.O. Box 416
Old Chelsea Station
New York, NY 10113-0416

or visit our website at:
www.cosimobooks.com

The Escape Or, A Leap for Freedom was originally published in 1858.

Cover design by www.kerndesign.net

ISBN: 978-1-60206-645-8

AUTHOR'S PREFACE.

THIS play was written for my own amusement, and not with the remotest thought that it would ever be seen by the public eye. I read it privately, however, to a circle of my friends, and through them was invited to read it before a Literary Society. Since then, the Drama has been given in various parts of the country. By the earnest solicitation of some in whose judgment I have the greatest confidence, I now present it in a printed form to the public. As I never aspired to be a dramatist, I ask no favor for it, and have little or no solicitude for its fate. If it is not readable, no word of mine can make it so; if it is, to ask favor for it would be needless.

The main features in the Drama are true. GLEN and MELINDA are actual characters, and still reside in Canada. Many of the incidents were drawn from my own experience of eighteen years at the South. The marriage ceremony, as performed in the second act, is still adhered to in many of the Southern States, especially in the farming districts.

The ignorance of the slave, as seen in the case of "BIG SALLY," is common wherever chattel slavery exists. The difficulties created in the domestic circle by the presence of beautiful slave women, as found in DR. GAINES'S family, is well understood by all who have ever visited the valley of the Mississippi.

The play, no doubt, abounds in defects, but as I was born in slavery, and never had a day's schooling in my life, I owe the public no apology for errors.

W. W. B.

CHARACTERS REPRESENTED.

DR. GAINES, *proprietor of the farm at Muddy Creek.*
REV. JOHN PINCHEN, *a clergyman.*
DICK WALKER, *a slave speculator.*
MR. WILDMARSH, *neighbor to Dr. Gaines.*
MAJOR MOORE, *a friend of Dr. Gaines.*
MR. WHITE, *a citizen of Massachusetts.*
BILL JENNINGS, *a slave speculator.*
JACOB SCRAGG, *overseer to Dr. Gaines.*
MRS. GAINES, *wife of Dr. Gaines.*
MR. and MRS. NEAL, and DAUGHTER, *Quakers, in Ohio.*
THOMAS, *Mr. Neal's hired man.*
GLEN, *slave of Mr. Hamilton, brother-in-law of Dr. Gaines.*
CATO, SAM, SAMPEY, MELINDA, DOLLY, SUSAN, and BIG SALLY,
slaves of Dr. Gaines.
PETE, NED, and BILL, *slaves.*
OFFICERS, LOUNGERS, BARKEEPER, &c.

THE ESCAPE.

ACT I.

Scene 1.—A SITTING-ROOM.

MRS. GAINES, *looking at some drawings*—SAMPEY, *a white slave, stands behind the lady's chair.*

Enter DR. GAINES, R.

Dr. Gaines. Well, my dear, my practice is steadily increasing. I forgot to tell you that neighbor Wyman engaged me yesterday as his family physician; and I hope that the fever and ague, which is now taking hold of the people, will give me more patients. I see by the New Orleans papers that the yellow fever is raging there to a fearful extent. Men of my profession are reaping a harvest in that section this year. I would that we could have a touch of the yellow fever here, for I think I could invent a medicine that would cure it. But the yellow fever is a luxury that we medical men in this climate can't expect to enjoy; yet we may hope for the cholera.

Mrs. Gaines. Yes, I would be glad to see it more sickly here, so that your business might prosper. But we are always unfortunate. Every body here seems to be in good health, and I am afraid that they 'll keep so. However, we must hope for the best. We must trust in the Lord. Providence may possibly send some disease amongst us for our benefit.

Enter Cato, r.

Cato. Mr. Campbell is at de door, massa.
Dr. G. Ask him in, Cato.

Enter Mr. Campbell, r.

Dr. G. Good morning, Mr. Campbell.   Be seated.
Mr. Campbell. Good morning, doctor.   The same to you,
Mrs. Gaines.   Fine morning, this.
Mrs. G. Yes, sir; beautiful day.
Mr. C. Well, doctor, I've come to engage you for my
family physician.   I am tired of Dr. Jones.   I've lost
another very valuable nigger under his treatment; and, as
my old mother used to say, " change of pastures makes fat
calves."
Dr. G. I shall be most happy to become your doctor.   Of
course, you want me to attend to your niggers, as well as to
your family ?
Mr. C. Certainly, sir.   I have twenty-three servants.
What will you charge me by the year ?
Dr. G. Of course, you'll do as my other patients do,
send your servants to me when they are sick, if able to
walk ?
Mr. C. Oh, yes; I always do that.
Dr. G. Then I suppose I'll have to lump it, and say
$500 per annum.
Mr. C. Well, then, we'll consider that matter settled;
and as two of the boys are sick, I'll send them over.   So
I'll bid you good day, doctor.   I would be glad if you
would come over some time, and bring Mrs. Gaines with
you.
Dr. G. Yes, I will; and shall be glad if you will pay us
a visit, and bring with you Mrs. Campbell.   Come over and
spend the day.
Mr. C. I will.   Good morning, doctor.

[*Exit* Mr. Campbell, r.

Dr. G. There, my dear, what do you think of that ?
Five hundred dollars more added to our income.   That's
patronage worth having !   And I am glad to get all the
negroes I can to doctor, for Cato is becoming very useful
to me in the shop.   He can bleed, pull teeth, and do almost

any thing that the blacks require. He can put up medicine as well as any one. A valuable boy, Cato!

Mrs. G. But why did you ask Mr. Campbell to visit you, and to bring his wife? I am sure I could never consent to associate with her, for I understand that she was the daughter of a tanner. You must remember, my dear, that I was born with a silver spoon in my mouth. The blood of the Wyleys runs in my veins. I am surprised that you should ask him to visit you at all; you should have known better.

Dr. G. Oh, I did not mean for him to visit me. I only invited him for the sake of compliments, and I think he so understood it; for I should be far from wishing you to associate with Mrs. Campbell. I don't forget, my dear, the family you were raised in, nor do I overlook my own family. My father, you know, fought by the side of Washington, and I hope some day to have a handle to my own name. I am certain Providence intended me for something higher than a medical man. Ah! by-the-by, I had forgotten that I have a couple of patients to visit this morning. I must go at once.　　　　　　　　　　[*Exit* Dr. Gaines, r.

Enter Hannah, l.

Mrs. G. Go, Hannah, and tell Dolly to kill a couple of fat pullets, and to put the biscuit to rise. I expect brother Pinchen here this afternoon, and I want every thing in order. Hannah, Hannah, tell Melinda to come here.

　　　　　　　　　　　　　　　　[*Exit* Hannah, l.

We mistresses do have a hard time in this world; I don't see why the Lord should have imposed such heavy duties on us poor mortals. Well, it can't last always. I long to leave this wicked world, and go home to glory.

Enter Melinda.

I am to have company this afternoon, Melinda. I expect brother Pinchen here, and I want every thing in order. Go and get one of my new caps, with the lace border, and get out my scolloped-bottomed dimity petticoat, and when you go out, tell Hannah to clean the white-handled knives, and see that not a speck is on them; for I want every thing as it should be while brother Pinchen is here.

　　　　　　　　　　　[*Exit* Mrs. Gaines, l, Hannah, r.

Scene 2.—DOCTOR'S SHOP—CATO MAKING PILLS.

Enter DR. GAINES, L.

Dr. G. Well, Cato, have you made the batch of ointment that I ordered?

Cato. Yes, massa; I dun made de intment, an' now I is making the bread pills. De tater pills is up on the top shelf.

Dr. G. I am going out to see some patients. If any gentlemen call, tell them I shall be in this afternoon. If any servants come, you attend to them. I expect two of Mr. Campbell's boys over. You see to them. Feel their pulse, look at their tongues, bleed them, and give them each a dose of calomel. Tell them to drink no cold water, and to take nothing but water gruel.

Cato. Yes, massa; I 'll tend to 'em.

[*Exit* DR. GAINES, L.

Cato. I allers knowed I was a doctor, an' now de ole boss has put me at it, I muss change my coat. Ef any niggers comes in, I wants to look suspectable. Dis jacket don't suit a doctor; I 'll change it. [*Exit* CATO—*immediately returning in a long coat.*] Ah! now I looks like a doctor. Now I can bleed, pull teef, or cut off a leg. Oh! well, well, ef I aint put de pill stuff an' de intment stuff togedder. By golly, dat ole cuss will be mad when he finds it out, won't he? Nebber mind, I 'll make it up in pills, and when de flour is on dem, he won't know what 's in 'em; an' I 'll make some new intment. Ah! yonder comes Mr. Campbell's Pete an' Ned; dems de ones massa sed was comin'. I 'll see ef I looks right. [*Goes to the looking-glass and views himself.*] I em some punkins, ain't I? [*Knock at the door.*] Come in.

Enter PETE *and* NED, R.

Pete. Whar is de doctor?

Cato. Here I is; don't you see me?

Pete. But whar is de ole boss?

Cato. Dat 's none you business. I dun tole you dat I is de doctor, an dat 's enuff.

Ned. Oh! do tell us whar de doctor is. I is almos dead. Oh me! oh dear me! I is so sick. [*Horrible faces.*]

Pete. Yes, do tell us; we don't want to stan here foolin'.

Cato. I tells you again dat I is de doctor. I larn de trade under massa.

Ned. Oh! well, den, give me somethin' to stop dis pain. Oh dear me! I shall die. [*He tries to vomit, but can't— ugly faces.*]

Cato. Let me feel your pulse. Now put out your tongue. You is berry sick. Ef you don't mine, you 'll die. Come out in de shed, an' I 'll bleed you.   [*Exit all—re-enter.*

Cato—Dar, now take dese pills, two in de mornin' and two at night, and ef you don't feel better, double de dose. Now, Mr. Pete, what's de matter wid you?

Pete. I is got de cole chills, an' has a fever in de night.

Cato. Come out, an' I 'll bleed you.   [*Exit all—re-enter.* Now take dese pills, two in de mornin' and two at night, an' ef dey don't help you, double de dose. Ah! I like to forget to feel your pulse and look at your tongue. Put out your tongue. [*Feels his pulse.*] Yes, I tells by de feel ob your pulse dat I is gib you de right pills.

Enter Mr. *Parker's* BILL, L.

Cato. What you come in dat door widout knockin' for?

Bill. My toof ache so, I didn't tink to knock. Oh, my toof! my toof! Whar is de doctor?

Cato. Here I is; don't you see me?

Bill. What! you de doctor, you brack cuss! You looks like a doctor! Oh, my toof! my toof! Whar is de doctor?

Cato. I tells you I is de doctor. Ef you don't believe me, ax dese men. I can pull your toof in a minnit.

Bill. Well, den, pull it out. Oh, my toof! how it aches! Oh, my toof! [*Cato gets the rusty turnkeys.*]

Cato. Now lay down on your back.

Bill. What for?

Cato. Dat 's de way massa does.

Bill. Oh, my toof! Well, den, come on. [*Lies down, Cato gets astraddle of Bill's breast, puts the turnkeys on the wrong tooth, and pulls—Bill kicks, and cries out*]— Oh, do stop! Oh! oh! oh! [*Cato pulls the wrong tooth— Bill jumps up.*

Cato. Dar, now, I tole you I could pull your toof for you.

Bill. Oh, dear me! Oh, it aches yet! Oh me! Oh, Lor-e-massy! You dun pull de wrong toof. Drat your skin! ef I don't pay you for this, you brack cuss! [*They fight, and turn over table, chairs and bench—Pete and Ned look on.*

Enter DR. GAINES, R.

Dr. G. Why, dear me, what's the matter? What's all this about? I'll teach you a lesson, that I will. [*The doctor goes at them with his cane.*

Cato. Oh, massa! he's to blame, sir. He's to blame. He struck me fuss.

Bill. No, sir; he's to blame; he pull de wrong toof. Oh, my toof! oh, my toof!

Dr. G. Let me see your tooth. Open your mouth. As I live, you've taken out the wrong tooth. I am amazed. I'll whip you for this; I'll whip you well. You're a pretty doctor. Now lie down, Bill, and let him take out the right tooth; and if he makes a mistake this time, I'll cowhide him well. Lie down, Bill. [*Bill lies down, and Cato pulls the tooth.*] There now, why didn't you do that in the first place?

Cato. He wouldn't hole still, sir.

Bill. He lies, sir. I did hole still.

Dr. G. Now go home, boys; go home.

[*Exit* PETE, NED *and* BILL, L.

Dr. G. You've made a pretty muss of it, in my absence. Look at the table! Never mind, Cato; I'll whip you well for this conduct of yours to-day. Go to work now, and clear up the office.   [*Exit* Dr. GAINES, R.

Cato. Confound dat nigger! I wish he was in Ginny. He bite my finger and scratch my face. But didn't I give it to him? Well, den, I reckon I did. [*He goes to the mirror, and discovers that his coat is torn—weeps.*] Oh, dear me! Oh, my coat—my coat is tore! Dat nigger has tore my coat. [*He gets angry, and rushes about the room frantic.*] Cuss dat nigger! Ef I could lay my hands on him, I'd tare him all to pieces,—dat I would. An' de ole boss hit me wid his cane after dat nigger tore my coat. By golly, I wants to fight somebody. Ef ole massa should come in now, I'd fight him. [*Rolls up his sleeves.*] Let 'em come now, ef dey dare—ole massa, or any body else; I'm ready for 'em.

Enter Dr. Gaines, r.

Dr. G. What's all this noise here?

Cato. Nuffin', sir; only jess I is puttin' things to rights, as you tole me. I didn't hear any noise except de rats.

Dr. G. Make haste, and come in; I want you to go to town.   [*Exit* Dr. Gaines, r.

Cato. By golly, de ole boss like to cotch me dat time, didn't he? But was n't I mad? When I is mad, nobody can do nuffin' wid me. But here's my coat, tore to pieces. Cuss dat nigger! [*Weeps.*] Oh, my coat! oh, my coat! I rudder he had broke my head den to tore my coat. Drat dat nigger! Ef he ever comes here agin, I'll pull out every toof he's got in his head—dat I will.   [*Exit*, r.

Scene 3.—A Room in the Quarters.

Enter Glen, l.

Glen. How slowly the time passes away. I've been waiting here two hours, and Melinda has not yet come. What keeps her, I cannot tell. I waited long and late for her last night, and when she approached, I sprang to my feet, caught her in my arms, pressed her to my heart, and kissed away the tears from her moistened cheeks. She placed her trembling hand in mine, and said, "Glen, I am yours; I will never be the wife of another." I clasped her to my bosom, and called God to witness that I would ever 'regard her as my wife. Old Uncle Joseph joined us in holy wedlock by moonlight; that was the only marriage ceremony. I look upon the vow as ever binding on me, for I am sure that a just God will sanction our union in heaven. Still, this man, who claims Melinda as his property, is unwilling for me to marry the woman of my choice, because he wants her himself. But he shall not have her. What he will say when he finds that we are married, I cannot tell; but I am determined to protect my wife or die. Ah! here comes Melinda.

Enter Melinda, r.

I am glad to see you, Melinda. I've been waiting long, and feared you would not come. Ah! in tears again?

Melinda. Glen, you are always thinking I am in tears. But what did master say to-day?

Glen. He again forbade our union.

Melinda. Indeed! Can he be so cruel?

Glen. Yes, he can be just so cruel.

Melinda. Alas! alas! how unfeeling and heartless! But did you appeal to his generosity?

Glen. Yes, I did; I used all the persuasive powers that I was master of, but to no purpose; he was inflexible. He even offered me a new suit of clothes, if I would give you up; and when I told him that I could not, he said he would flog me to death if I ever spoke to you again.

Melinda. And what did you say to him?

Glen. I answered, that, while I loved life better than death, even life itself could not tempt me to consent to a separation that would make life an unchanging curse. Oh, I would kill myself, Melinda, if I thought that, for the sake of life, I could consent to your degradation. No, Melinda, I can die, but shall never live to see you the mistress of another man. But, my dear girl, I have a secret to tell you, and no one must know it but you. I will go out and see that no person is within hearing. I will be back soon.

[*Exit* Glen, L.

Melinda. It is often said that the darkest hour of the night precedes the dawn. It is ever thus with the vicissitudes of human suffering. After the soul has reached the lowest depths of despair, and can no deeper plunge amid its rolling, fœtid shades, then the reactionary forces of man's nature begin to operate, resolution takes the place of despondency, energy succeeds instead of apathy, and an upward tendency is felt and exhibited. Men then hope against power, and smile in defiance of despair. I shall never forget when first I saw Glen. It is now more than a year since he came here with his master, Mr. Hamilton. It was a glorious moonlight night in autumn. The wide and fruitful face of nature was silent and buried in repose. The tall trees on the borders of Muddy Creek waved their leafy branches in the breeze, which was wafted from afar, refreshing over hill and vale, over the rippling water, and the waving corn and wheat fields. The starry sky was studded over with a few light, flitting clouds, while the moon, as if rejoicing to witness the meeting of two hearts that should be cemented by the purest love, sailed triumphantly along among the shifting vapors.

Oh, how happy I have been in my acquaintance with Glen! That he loves me, I do well believe it; that I love him, it is most true. Oh, how I would that those who think the slave incapable of the finer feelings, could only see our hearts, and learn our thoughts,—thoughts that we dare not utter in the presence of our masters! But I fear that Glen will be separated from me, for there is nothing too base and mean for master to do, for the purpose of getting me entirely in his power. But, thanks to Heaven, he does not own Glen, and therefore cannot sell him. Yet he might purchase him from his brother-in-law, so as to send him out of the way. But here comes my husband.

Enter Glen, l.

Glen. I've been as far as the overseer's house, and all is quiet. Now, Melinda, as you are my wife, I will confide to you a secret. I've long been thinking of making my escape to Canada, and taking you with me. It is true that I don't belong to your master, but he might buy me from Hamilton, and then sell me out of the neighborhood.

Melinda. But we could never succeed in the attempt to escape.

Glen. We will make the trial, and show that we at least deserve success. There is a slave trader expected here next week, and Dr. Gaines would sell you at once if he knew that we were married. We must get ready and start, and if we can pass the Ohio river, we'll be safe on the road to Canada.   [*Exit*, r.

*Scene 4.—*Dining-Room.

Rev. Mr. Pinchen *giving* Mrs. Gaines *an account of his experience as a minister—*Hannah *clearing away the breakfast table—*Sampey *standing behind* Mrs. Gaines' *chair.*

Mrs. Gaines. Now, do give me more of your experience, brother Pinchen. It always does my soul good to hear religious experience. It draws me nearer and nearer to the Lord's side. I do love to hear good news from God's people.

Mr. Pinchen. Well, sister Gaines, I've had great opportunities in my time to study the heart of man. I've attended a great many camp-meetings, revival meetings, protracted meetings, and death-bed scenes, and I am satisfied, sister Gaines, that the heart of man is full of sin, and desperately wicked. This is a wicked world, sister Gaines, a wicked world.

Mrs. G. Were you ever in Arkansas, brother Pinchen? I've been told that the people out there are very ungodly.

Mr. P. Oh, yes, sister Gaines. I once spent a year at Little Rock, and preached in all the towns round about there; and I found some hard cases out there, I can tell you. I was once spending a week in a district where there were a great many horse thieves, and one night, somebody stole my pony. Well, I knowed it was no use to make a fuss, so I told brother Tarbox to say nothing about it, and I'd get my horse by preaching God's everlasting gospel; for I had faith in the truth, and knowed that my Savior would not let me lose my pony. So the next Sunday I preached on horse-stealing, and told the brethren to come up in the evenin' with their hearts filled with the grace of God. So that night the house was crammed brim full with anxious souls, panting for the bread of life. Brother Bingham opened with prayer, and brother Tarbox followed, and I saw right off that we were gwine to have a blessed time. After I got 'em pretty well warmed up, I jumped on to one of the seats, stretched out my hands, and said, "I know who stole my pony; I've found out; and you are in here tryin' to make people believe that you've got religion; but you ain't got it. And if you don't take my horse back to brother Tarbox's pasture this very night, I'll tell your name right out in meetin' to-morrow night. Take my pony back, you vile and wretched sinner, and come up here and give your heart to God." So the next mornin', I went out to brother Tarbox's pasture, and sure enough, there was my bob-tail pony. Yes, sister Gaines, there he was, safe and sound. Ha, ha, ha.

Mrs. G. Oh, how interesting, and how fortunate for you to get your pony! And what power there is in the gospel! God's children are very lucky. Oh, it is so sweet to sit here and listen to such good news from God's people! You Hannah, what are you standing there listening for, and neglecting your work? Never mind, my lady, I'll whip you

well when I am done here.   Go at your work this moment,
you lazy huzzy!   Never mind, I 'll whip you well. [*Aside.*]
Come, do go on, brother Pinchen, with your godly conversation.   It is so sweet!   It draws me nearer and nearer to
the Lord's side.

Mr. P. Well, sister Gaines, I 've had some mighty queer
dreams in my time, that I have.   You see, one night I
dreamed that I was dead and in heaven, and such a place I
never saw before.   As soon as I entered the gates of the
celestial empire, I saw many old and familiar faces that I
had seen before.   The first person that I saw was good old
Elder Pike, the preacher that first called my attention to
religion.   The next person I saw was Deacon Billings, my
first wife's father, and then I saw a host of godly faces.
Why, sister Gaines, you knowed Elder Goosbee, didn't
you?

Mrs. G. Why, yes; did you see him there?   He married me to my first husband.

Mr. P. Oh, yes, sister Gaines, I saw the old Elder, and
he looked for all the world as if he had just come out of a
revival meetin'.

Mrs. G. Did you see my first husband there, brother
Pinchen?

Mr. P. No, sister Gaines, I didn't see brother Pepper
there; but I 've no doubt but that brother Pepper was there.

Mrs. G. Well, I don't know; I have my doubts.   He
was not the happiest man in the world.   He was always
borrowing trouble about something or another.   Still, I saw
some happy moments with Mr. Pepper.   I was happy when
I made his acquaintance, happy during our courtship, happy
a while after our marriage, and happy when he died.
[*Weeps.*]

Hannah. Massa Pinchen, did you see my ole man Ben up
dar in hebben?

Mr. P. No, Hannah; I didn't go amongst the niggers.

Mrs. G. No, of course brother Pinchen didn't go among
the blacks.   What are you asking questions for?   Never
mind, my lady, I 'll whip you well when I 'm done here.
I 'll skin you from head to foot.   [*Aside.*]   Do go on with
your heavenly conversation, brother Pinchen; it does my
very soul good.   This is indeed a precious moment for me.
I do love to hear of Christ and Him crucified.

Mr. P. Well, sister Gaines, I promised sister Daniels that I'd come over and see her this morning, and have a little season of prayer with her, and I suppose I must go. I'll tell you more of my religious experience when I return.

Mrs. G. If you must go, then I'll have to let you; but before you do, I wish to get your advice upon a little matter that concerns Hannah. Last week, Hannah stole a goose, killed it, cooked it, and she and her man Sam had a fine time eating the goose; and her master and I would never have known a word about it, if it had not been for Cato, a faithful servant, who told his master. And then, you see, Hannah had to be severely whipped before she'd confess that she stole the goose. Next Sabbath is sacrament day, and I want to know if you think that Hannah is fit to go to the Lord's supper after stealing the goose.

Mr. P. Well, sister Gaines, that depends on circumstances. If Hannah has confessed that she stole the goose, and has been sufficiently whipped, and has begged her master's pardon, and begged your pardon, and thinks she'll never do the like again, why then I suppose she can go to the Lord's supper; for

> "While the lamp holds out to burn,
> The vilest sinner may return."

But she must be sure that she has repented, and won't steal any more.

Mrs. G. Now, Hannah, do you hear that? For my own part, I don't think she's fit to go to the Lord's supper, for she had no occasion to steal the goose. We give our niggers plenty of good wholesome food. They have a full run to the meal tub, meat once a fortnight, and all the sour milk about the place, and I'm sure that's enough for any one. I do think that our niggers are the most ungrateful creatures in the world, that I do. They aggravate my life out of me.

Hannah. I know, missis, dat I steal de goose, and massa whip me for it, and I confess it, and I is sorry for it. But, missis, I is gwine to de Lord's supper, next Sunday, kase I ain't agwine to turn my back on my bressed Lord an' Massa for no old tough goose, dat I ain't. [*Weeps.*]

Mr. P. Well, sister Gaines, I suppose I must go over and see sister Daniels; she'll be waiting for me.

[*Exit* MR. PINCHEN, M. D.

Mrs. G. Now, Hannah, brother Pinchen is gone, do you
get the cowhide and follow me to the cellar, and I'll whip
you well for aggravating me as you have to-day.   It seems
as if I can never sit down to take a little comfort with the
Lord, without you crossing me.   The devil always puts it
into your head to disturb me, just when I am trying to
serve the Lord.   I've no doubt but that I'll miss going to
heaven on your account.   But I'll whip you well before I
leave this world, that I will.   Get the cowhide and follow
me to the cellar.

[*Exit* MRS. GAINES *and* HANNAH, R.

ACT II.

Scene 1.—PARLOR.

DR. GAINES *at a table, letters and papers before him.*

Enter SAMPEY, L.

Sampey. Dar's a gemman at de doe, massa, dat wants to
see you, seer.

Dr. Gaines. Ask him to walk in, Sampey.

[*Exit* SAMPEY, L.

Enter WALKER.

Walker. Why, how do you do, Dr. Gaines?   I em glad
to see you, I'll swear.

Dr. G. How do you do, Mr. Walker?   I did not expect
to see you up here so soon.   What has hurried you?

Walk. Well, you see, doctor, I comes when I em not
expected.   The price of niggers is up, and I em gwine to
take advantage of the times.   Now, doctor, ef you've got
any niggers that you wants to sell, I em your man.   I am
paying the highest price of any body in the market.   I
pay cash down, and no grumblin'.

Dr. G. I don't know that I want to sell any of my people now.   Still, I've got to make up a little money next
month, to pay in bank; and another thing, the doctors say
that we are likely to have a touch of the cholera this sum-

mer, and if that's the case, I suppose I had better turn as many of my slaves into cash as I can.

Walk. Yes, doctor, that is very true. The cholera is death on slaves, and a thousand dollars in your pocket is a great deal better than a nigger in the field, with cholera at his heels. Why, who is that coming up the lane? It's Mr. Wildmarsh, as I live! Jest the very man I wants to see.

Enter Mr. WILDMARSH.

Why, how do you do, Squire? I was jest a thinkin' about you.

Wildmarsh. How are you, Mr. Walker? and how are you, doctor? I am glad to see you both looking so well. You seem in remarkably good health, doctor?

Dr. G. Yes, Squire, I was never in the enjoyment of better health. I hope you left all well at Licking?

Wild. Yes, I thank you. And now, Mr. Walker, how goes times with you?

Walk. Well, you see, Squire, I em in good spirits. The price of niggers is up in the market, and I am lookin' out for bargains; and I was jest intendin' to come over to Lickin' to see you, to see if you had any niggers to sell. But it seems as ef the Lord knowed that I wanted to see you, and directed your steps over here. Now, Squire, ef you 've got any niggers you wants to sell, I em your man. I am payin' the highest cash price of any body in the market. Now 's your time, Squire.

Wild. No, I don't think I want to sell any of my slaves now. I sold a very valuable gal to Mr. Haskins last week. I tell you, she was a smart one. I got eighteen hundred dollars for her.

Walk. Why, Squire, how you do talk! Eighteen hundred dollars for one gal? She must have been a screamer to bring that price. What sort of a lookin' critter was she? I should like to have bought her.

Wild. She was a little of the smartest gal I 've ever raised; that she was.

Walk. Then she was your own raising, was she?

Wild. Oh, yes; she was raised on my place, and if I could have kept her three or four years longer, and taken her to the market myself, I am sure I could have sold her for three thousand dollars. But you see, Mr. Walker, my wife got a little jealous, and you know jealousy sets the women's heads a teetering, and so I had to sell the gal. She's got straight hair, blue eyes, prominent features, and is almost white. Haskins will make a spec, and no mistake.

Walk. Why, Squire, was she that pretty little gal that I saw on your knee the day that your wife was gone, when I was at your place three years ago?

Wild. Yes, the same.

Walk. Well, now, Squire, I thought that was your daughter; she looked mightily like you. She was your daughter, was n't she? You need not be ashamed to own it to me, for I am mum upon such matters.

Wild. You know, Mr. Walker, that people will talk, and when they talk, they say a great deal; and people did talk, and many said the gal was my daughter; and you know we can't help people's talking. But here comes the Rev. Mr. Pinchen; I didn't know that he was in the neighborhood.

Walk. It is Mr. Pinchen, as I live; jest the very man I wants to see.

Enter Mr. Pinchen, r.

Why, how do you do, Mr. Pinchen? What in the name of Jehu brings you down here to Muddy Creek? Any camp-meetins, revival meetins, death-bed scenes, or any .thing else in your line going on down here? How is religion prosperin' now, Mr. Pinchen? I always like to hear about religion.

Mr. Pin. Well, Mr. Walker, the Lord's work is in good condition every where now. I tell you, Mr. Walker, I've been in the gospel ministry these thirteen years, and I am satisfied that the heart of man is full of sin and desperately wicked. This is a wicked world, Mr. Walker, a wicked world, and we ought all of us to have religion. Religion is a good thing to live by, and we all want it when we die. Yes, sir, when the great trumpet blows, we ought to be ready. And a man in your business of buying and selling slaves needs religion more than any body else, for it makes you treat your people as you should. Now, there is Mr. Haskins,—he is a slave-trader, like yourself. Well, I converted him. Before he got religion, he was one of the worst men to his niggers I ever saw; his heart was as hard as stone. But religion has made his heart as soft as a piece of cotton. Before I converted him, he would sell husbands from their wives, and seem to take delight in it; but now he won't sell a man from his wife, if he can get any one to buy both of them together. I tell you, sir, religion has done a wonderful work for him.

Walk. I know, Mr. Pinchen, that I ought to have religion, and I feel that I am a great sinner; and whenever I get with good pious people like you and the doctor, and Mr. Wildmarsh, it always makes me feel that I am a desperate sinner. I feel it the more, because I've got a religious turn of mind. I know that I would be happier with religion, and the first spare time I get, I am going to try to get it. I'll go to a protracted meeting, and I won't stop till I get religion. Yes, I'll scuffle with the Lord till I gets forgiven. But it always makes me feel bad to talk about religion, so I'll change the subject. Now, doctor, what about them thar niggers you thought you could sell me?

Dr. Gaines. I'll see my wife, Mr. Walker, and if she is willing to part with Hannah, I'll sell you Sam and his wife, Hannah. Ah! here comes my wife; I'll mention it.

Enter MRS. GAINES, L.

Ah! my dear, I am glad you've come. I was just telling Mr. Walker, that if you were willing to part with Hannah, I'd sell him Sam and Hannah.

Mrs. G. Now, Dr. Gaines, I am astonished and surprised that you should think of such a thing. You know what trouble I've had in training up Hannah for a house servant, and now that I've got her so that she knows my ways, you want to sell her. Havn't you niggers enough on the plantation to sell, without selling the servants from under very nose?

Dr. G. Oh, yes, my dear; but I can spare Sam, and don't like to separate him from his wife; and I thought if you could let Hannah go, I'd sell them both. I don't like to separate husbands from their wives.

Mrs. G. Now, gentlemen, that's just the way with my husband. He thinks more about the welfare and comfort of his slaves, than he does of himself or his family. I am sure you need not feel so bad at the thought of separating Sam from Hannah. They've only been married eight

months, and their attachment can't be very strong in that
short time.   Indeed, I shall be glad if you do sell Sam, for
then I'll make Hannah *jump the broomstick* with Cato, and
I'll have them both here under my eye.   I never will again
let one of my house servants marry a field hand—never!
For when night comes on, the servants are off to the quar-
ters, and I have to holler and holler enough to split my
throat before I can make them hear.   And another thing: I
want you to sell Melinda.   I don't intend to keep that mulat-
to wench about the house any longer.

Dr. Gaines. My dear, I'll sell any servant from the place
to suit you, except Melinda.   I can't think of selling her—I
can't think of it.

Mrs. G. I tell you that Melinda shall leave this house, or
I'll go.   There, now you have it.   I've had my life tor-
mented out of me by the presence of that yellow wench, and
I'll stand it no longer.   I know you love her more than you
do me, and I'll—I'll—I'll write—write to my father.
[*Weeps.*]   [*Exit* Mrs. Gaines, l.

Walk. Why, doctor, your wife's a screamer, ain't she ?
Ha, ha, ha.   Why, doctor, she's got a tongue of her own,
ain't she ?   Why, doctor, it was only last week that I thought
of getting a wife myself; but your wife has skeered the idea
out of my head.   Now, doctor, if you wants to sell the gal,
I'll buy her.   Husband and wife ought to be on good terms,
and your wife won't feel well till the gal is gone.   Now,
I'll pay you all she's worth, if you wants to sell.

Dr. G. No, Mr. Walker; the girl my wife spoke of is
not for sale.   My wife does not mean what she says; she's
only a little jealous.   I'll get brother Pinchen to talk to
her, and get her mind turned upon religious matters, and
then she'll forget it.   She's only a little jealous.

Walk. I tell you what, doctor, ef you call that a little
jealous, I'd like to know what's a heap.   I tell you, it will
take something more than religion to set your wife right.
You had better sell me the gal; I'll pay you cash down, and
no grumblin'.

Dr. G. The girl is not for sale, Mr. Walker; but if you
want two good, able-bodied servants, I'll sell you Sam and
Big Sally.   Sam is trustworthy, and Sally is worth her
weight in gold for rough usage.

Walk. Well, doctor, I'll go out and take a look at 'em, for I never buys slaves without examining them well, because they are sometimes injured by over-work or under-feedin'. I don't say that is the case with yours, for I don't believe it is; but as I sell on honor, I must buy on honor.

Dr. G. Walk out, sir, and you can examine them to your heart's content. Walk right out, sir.

Scene 2.—VIEW IN FRONT OF THE GREAT HOUSE.

Examination of SAM *and* BIG SALLY.—DR. GAINES, WILD-MARSH, MR. PINCHEN *and* WALKER *present.*

Walk. Well, my boy, what's your name?

Sam. Sam, sir, is my name.

Walk. How old are you, Sam?

Sam. Ef I live to see next corn plantin' time, I'll be 27, or 30, or 35, or 40—I don't know which, sir.

Walk. Ha, ha, ha. Well, doctor, this is rather a green boy. Well, mer feller, are you sound?

Sam. Yes, sir, I spec I is.

Walk. Open your mouth and let me see your teeth. I allers judge a nigger's age by his teeth, same as I dose a hoss. Ah! pretty good set of grinders. Have you got a good appetite?

Sam. Yes, sir.

Walk. Can you eat your allowance?

Sam. Yes, sir, when I can get it.

Walk. Get out on the floor and dance; I want to see if you are supple.

Sam. I don't like to dance; I is got religion.

Walk. Oh, ho! you've got religion, have you? That's so much the better. I likes to deal in the gospel. I think he'll suit me. Now, mer gal, what's your name?

Sally. I is Big Sally, sir.

Walk. How old are you, Sally?

Sally. I don't know, sir; but I heard once dat I was born at sweet pertater diggin' time.

Walk. Ha, ha, ha. Don't know how old you are! Do you know who made you?

Sally. I hev heard who it was in de Bible dat made me, but I dun forget de gentman's name.

Walk. Ha, ha, ha. Well, doctor, this is the greenest lot of niggers I've seen for some time. Well, what do you ask for them?

Dr. Gaines. You may have Sam for $1000, and Sally for $900. They are worth all I ask for them. You know I never banter, Mr. Walker. There they are; you can take them at that price, or let them alone, just as you please.

Walk. Well, doctor, I reckon I'll take 'em; but it's all they are worth. I'll put the handcuffs on 'em, and then I'll pay you. I likes to go accordin' to Scripter. Scripter says ef eatin' meat will offend your brother, you must quit it; and I say, ef leavin' your slaves without the handcuffs will make 'em run away, you must put the handcuffs on 'em. Now, Sam, don't you and Sally cry. I am of a tender heart, and it allers makes me feel bad to see people cryin'. Don't cry, and the first place I get to, I'll buy each of you a great big *ginger cake*,—that I will. Now, Mr. Pinchen, I wish you were going down the river. I'd like to have your company; for I allers likes the company of preachers.

Mr. Pinchen. Well, Mr. Walker, I would be much pleased to go down the river with you, but it's too early for me. I expect to go to Natchez in four or five weeks, to attend a camp-meetin', and if you were going down then, I'd like it. What kind of niggers sells best in the Orleans market, Mr. Walker?

Walk. Why, field hands. Did you think of goin' in the trade?

Mr. P. Oh, no; only it's a long ways down to Natchez, and I thought I'd just buy five or six niggers, and take 'em down and sell 'em to pay my travellin' expenses. I only want to clear my way.

Scene 3.—Sitting-Room—Table and Rocking-Chair.

Enter Mrs. Gaines, r, *followed by* Sampey.

Mrs. Gaines. I do wish your master would come; I want supper. Run to the gate, Sampey, and see if he is coming.

[*Exit* Sampey, l.

That man is enough to break my heart. The patience of an angel could not stand it.

Enter Sampey, l.

Samp. Yes, missis, master is coming.

Enter DR. GAINES, L.

[*The Doctor walks about with his hands under his coat, seeming very much elated.*]

Mrs. Gaines. Why, doctor, what is the matter?

Dr. Gaines. My dear, don't call me *doctor*.

Mrs. G. What should I call you?

Dr. G. Call me Colonel, my dear—Colonel. I have been elected Colonel of the Militia, and I want you to call me by my right name. I always felt that Providence had designed me for something great, and He has just begun to shower His blessings upon me.

Mrs. G. Dear me, I could never get to calling you Colonel; I've called you Doctor for the last twenty years.

Dr. G. Now, Sarah, if you will call me Colonel, other people will, and I want you to set the example. Come, my darling, call me Colonel, and I'll give you any thing you wish for.

Mrs. G. Well, as I want a new gold watch and bracelets, I'll commence now. Come, Colonel, we'll go to supper. Ah! now for my new shawl. [*Aside.*] Mrs. Lemme was here to-day, Colonel, and she had on, Colonel, one of the prettiest shawls, Colonel, I think, Colonel, that I ever saw, Colonel, in my life, Colonel. And there is only one, Colonel, in Mr. Watson's store, Colonel; and that, Colonel, will do, Colonel, for a Colonel's wife.

Dr. G. Ah! my dear, you never looked so much the lady since I've known you. Go, my darling, get the watch, bracelets and shawl, and tell them to charge them to Colonel Gaines; and when you say "Colonel," always emphasize the word.

Mrs. G. Come, Colonel, let's go to supper.

Dr. G. My dear, you're a jewel,—you are!   [*Exit,* R.

Enter CATO, L.

Cato. Why, whar is massa and missis? I tought dey was here. Ah! by golly, yonder comes a mulatter gal. Yes, it's Mrs. Jones's Tapioca. I'll set up to dat gal, dat I will.

Enter TAPIOCA, R.

Good ebenin', Miss Tappy. How is your folks?

Tapioca. Pretty well, I tank you.

Cato. Miss Tappy, dis wanderin' heart of mine is yours. Come, take a seat! Please to squze my manners; love discommodes me. Take a seat. Now, Miss Tappy, I loves you; an ef you will jess marry me, I'll make you a happy husband, dat I will. Come, take me as I is.

Tap. But what will Big Jim say?

Cato. Big Jim! Why, let dat nigger go to Ginny. I want to know, now, if you is tinkin' about dat common nigger? Why, Miss Tappy, I is surstonished dat you should tink 'bout frowin' yousef away wid a common, ugly lookin' cuss like Big Jim, when you can get a fine lookin', suspectable man like me. Come, Miss Tappy, choose dis day who you have. Afore I go any furder, give me one kiss. Come, give me one kiss. Come, let me kiss you.

Tap. No you shan't—dare now! You shan't kiss me widout you is stronger den I is; and I know you is dat. [*He kisses her.*]

Enter DR. GAINES, R, *and hides.*

Cato. Did you know, Miss Tappy, dat I is de head doctor 'bout dis house? I beats de ole boss all to pieces.

Tap. I hev hearn dat you bleeds and pulls teef.

Cato. Yes, Miss Tappy; massa could not get along widout me, for massa was made a doctor by books; but I is a natral doctor. I was born a doctor, jess as Lorenzo Dow was born a preacher. So you see I can't be nuffin' but a doctor, while massa is a bunglin' ole cuss at de bissness.

Dr. Gaines, (in a low voice.) Never mind; I'll teach you a lesson, that I will.

Cato. You see, Miss Tappy, I was gwine to say——Ah! but afore I forget, jess give me anudder kiss, jess to keep company wid de one dat you give me jess now,—dat's all. [*Kisses her.*] Now, Miss Tappy, duse you know de fuss time dat I seed you?

Tap. No, Mr. Cato, I don't.

Cato. Well, it was at de camp-meetin'. Oh, Miss Tappy, dat pretty red calliker dress you had on dat time did de work for me. It made my heart flutter—

Dr. G. (low voice.) Yes, and I'll make your black hide flutter.

Cato. Didn't I hear some noise? By golly, dar is teves

in dis house, and I 'll drive 'em out. [*Takes a chair and runs at the Doctor, and knocks him down. The Doctor chases Cato round the table.*

Cato. Oh, massa, I didn't know 'twas you!

Dr. G. You scoundrel! I'll whip you well. Stop! I tell you.   [*Curtain falls.*

ACT III.

Scene 1.—SITTING-ROOM.

MRS. GAINES, *seated in an arm chair, reading a letter.*

Enter HANNAH, L.

Mrs. Gaines. You need not tell me, Hannah, that you don't want another husband, I know better. Your master has sold Sam, and he's gone down the river, and you'll never see him again. So, go and put on your calico dress, and meet me in the kitchen. I intend for you to *jump the broomstick* with Cato. You need not tell me that you don't want another man. I know that there's no woman living that can be happy and satisfied without a husband.

Hannah. Oh, missis, I don't want to jump de broomstick wid Cato. I don't love Cato; I can't love him.

Mrs. G. Shut up, this moment! What do you know about love? I didn't love your master when I married him, and people don't marry for love now. So go and put on your calico dress, and meet me in the kitchen.

[*Exit* HANNAH, L.

I am glad that the Colonel has sold Sam; now I'll make Hannah marry Cato, and I have them both here under my eye. And I am also glad that the Colonel has parted with Melinda. Still, I'm afraid that he is trying to deceive me. He took the hussy away yesterday, and says he sold her to a trader; but I don't believe it. At any rate, if she's in the neighborhood, I'll find her, that I will. No man ever fools me.   [*Exit* MRS. GAINES, L.

Scene 2.—The Kitchen—Slaves at Work.

Enter Hannah, R.

Hannah. Oh, Cato, do go and tell missis dat you don't want to jump de broomstick wid me,—dat's a good man! Do, Cato; kase I nebber can love you. It was only las week dat massa sold my Sammy, and I don't want any udder man. Do go tell missis dat you don't want me.

Cato. No, Hannah, I ain't a gwine to tell missis no such thing, kase I dose want you, and I ain't a-gwine to tell a lie for you ner nobody else. Dar, now you's got it! I don't see why you need to make so much fuss. I is better lookin' den Sam; an' I is a house servant, an' Sam was only a fiel hand; so you ought to feel proud of a change. So go and do as missis tells you.   [*Exit* Hannah, L.

Hannah needn't try to get me to tell a lie; I ain't a-gwine to do it, kase I dose want her, an' I is bin wantin' her dis long time, an' soon as massa sold Sam, I knowed I would get her. By golly, I is gwine to be a married man. Won't I be happy! Now, ef I could only jess run away from ole massa, an' get to Canada wid Hannah, den I'd show 'em who I was. Ah! dat reminds me of my song 'bout ole massa and Canada, an' I'll sing it fer yer. Dis is my moriginal hyme. It comed into my head one night when I was fass asleep under an apple tree, looking up at de moon. Now for my song :—

AIR—"*Dandy Jim.*"

Come all ye bondmen far and near,
Let's put a song in massa's ear,
It is a song for our poor race,
Who're whipped and trampled with disgrace.

CHORUS.

My old massa tells me, Oh,
This is a land of freedom, Oh;
Let's look about and see if it's so,
Just as massa tells me, Oh.

He tells us of that glorious one,
I think his name was Washington,
How he did fight for liberty,
To save a threepence tax on tea.   [*Chorus.*]

But now we look about and see
That we poor blacks are not so free;

We 're whipped and thrashed about like fools,
And have no chance at common schools. [*Chorus.*]

They take our wives, insult and mock,
And sell our children on the block,
They choke us if we say a word,
And say that "niggers" shan't be heard. [*Chorus.*]

Our preachers, too, with whip and cord,
Command obedience in the Lord;
They say they learn it from the big book,
But for ourselves, we dare not look. [*Chorus.*]

There is a country far away,
I think they call it Canada,
And if we reach Victoria's shore,
They say that we are slaves no more.

> Now haste, all bondmen, let us go,
> And leave this *Christian* country, Oh;
> Haste to the land of the British Queen,
> Where whips for negroes are not seen.

Now, if we go, we must take the night,
And never let them come in sight;
The bloodhounds will be on our track,
And wo to us if they fetch us back.

> Now haste all bondmen, let us go,
> And leave this *Christian* country, Oh;
> God help us to Victoria's shore,
> Where we are free and slaves no more!

Enter MRS. GAINES, L.

Mrs. Gaines. Ah! Cato, you 're ready, are you? Where is Hannah?

Cato. Yes, missis; I is bin waitin' dis long time. Hannah has bin here tryin' to swade me to tell you dat I do n't want her; but I telled her dat you sed I must jump de broomstick wid her, an' I is gwine to mind you.

Mrs. G. That's right, Cato; servants should always mind their masters and mistresses, without asking a question.

Cato. Yes, missis, I allers dose what you and massa tells me, an' axes nobody.

Enter HANNAH, R.

Mrs. Gaines. Ah! Hannah; come, we are waiting for you. Nothing can be done till you come.

Hannah. Oh, missis, I do n't want to jump de broomstick wid Cato; I can't love him.

Mrs. G. Shut up, this moment. Dolly, get the broom. Susan, you take hold of the other end. There, now hold it a little lower — there, a little higher. There, now, that'll do. Now Hannah, take hold of Cato's hand. Let Cato take hold of your hand.

Hannah. Oh, missis, do spare me. I do n't want to jump de broomstick wid Cato.

Mrs. G. Get the cowhide, and follow me to the cellar, and I 'll whip you well. I 'll let you know how to disobey my orders. Get the cowhide, and follow me to the cellar.   [*Exit* Mrs. Gaines *and* Hannah, R.

Dolly. Oh, Cato, do go an' tell missis dat you do n't want Hannah. Do n't you hear how she 's whippin' her in de cellar? Do go an' tell missis dat you do n't want Hannah, and den she 'll stop whippin' her.

Cato. No, Dolly, I ain't a-gwine to do no such a thing, kase ef I tell missis dat I do n't want Hannah, den missis will whip me; an' I ain't a-gwine to be whipped fer you, ner Hannah, ner nobody else. No, I 'll jump de broomstick wid every woman on de place, ef missis wants me to, before I 'll be whipped.

Dolly. Cato, ef I was in Hannah's place, I 'd see you in de bottomless pit before I 'd live wid you, you great big wall-eyed, empty-headed, knock-kneed fool. You're as mean as your devilish old missis.

Cato. Ef you do n't quit dat busin' me, Dolly, I 'll tell missis as soon as she comes in, an' she 'll whip you, you know she will.

Enter Mrs. Gaines *and* Hannah, R.

[*Mrs. G. fans herself with her handkerchief, and appears fatigued.*]

Mrs. G. You ought to be ashamed of yourself, Hannah, to make me fatigue myself in this way, to make you do your duty. It 's very naughty in you, Hannah. Now, Dolly, you and Susan get the broom, and get out in the middle of the room. There, hold it a little lower — a little higher; there, that 'll do. Now, remember that this is a solemn occasion; you are going to jump into matrimony. Now,

2

Cato, take hold of Hannah's hand. There, now, why couldn't you let Cato take hold of your hand before? Now get ready, and when I count three, do you jump. Eyes on the *broomstick!* All ready. One, two, three, and over you go. There, now you're husband and wife, and if you don't live happy together, it's your own fault; for I am sure (there's nothing to hinder it. Now, Hannah, come up to the house, and I'll give you some whiskey, and you can make some apple toddy, and you and Cato can have a fine time.   [*Exit* MRS. GAINES *and* HANNAH, L.

Dolly. I tell you what, Susan, when I get married, I is gwine to have a preacher to marry me. I ain't a-gwine to jump de broomstick. Dat will do for fiel' hands, but house servants ought to be 'bove dat.

Susan. Well, chile, you can't speck any ting else from ole missis. She come from down in Carlina, from 'mong de poor white trash. She don't know any better. You can't speck nothin' more dan a jump from a frog. Missis says she is one of de akastocacy; but she ain't no more of an akastocacy dan I is. Missis says she was born wid a silver spoon in her mouf; ef she was, I wish it had a-choked her, dat's what I wish. Missis wanted to make Linda jump de broomstick wid Glen, but massa ain't a-gwine to let Linda jump de broomstick wid anybody. He's gwine to keep Linda fer heself.

Dolly. You know massa took Linda 'way las' night, an' tell missis dat he has sold her and sent her down de river; but I don't b'lieve he has sold her at all. He went ober towards de poplar farm, an' I tink Linda is ober dar now. Ef she is dar, missis'll find it out, fer she tell'd massa las' night, dat ef Linda was in de neighborhood, she'd find her.
    [*Exit* DOLLY *and* SUSAN.

Scene 3.—SITTING ROOM—CHAIRS AND TABLE.
Enter HANNAH, R.

Hannah. I don't keer what missis says; I don't like Cato, an' I won't live wid him. I always love my Sammy, an' I loves him now. [*Knock at the door—goes to the door.*

Enter MAJ. MOORE, M. D.

Walk in, sir; take a seat. I'll call missis, sir; massa is gone away.   [*Exit* HANNAH, R.

Maj. Moore. So I am here at last, and the Colonel is not at home. I hope his wife is a good-looking woman. I rather like fine looking-women, especially when their husbands are from home. Well, I've studied human nature to some purpose. If you wish to get the good will of a man, don't praise his wife, and if you wish to gain the favor of a woman, praise her children, and swear that they are the picture of their father, whether they are or not. Ah! here comes the lady.

Enter Mrs. Gaines, r.

Mrs. G. Good morning, sir!

Maj. M. Good morning, madam! I am Maj. Moore, of Jefferson. The Colonel and I had seats near each other in the last Legislature.

Mrs. G. Be seated, sir. I think I've heard the Colonel speak of you. He's away, now; but I expect him every moment. You're a stranger here, I presume?

Maj. M. Yes, madam, I am. I rather like the Colonel's situation here.

Mrs. G. It is thought to be a fine location.

Enter Sampey, r.

Hand me my fan, will you, Sampey? [*Sampey gets the fan and passes near the Major, who mistakes the boy for the Colonel's son. He reaches out his hand.*

Maj. M. How do you do, bub? Madam, I should have known that this was the Colonel's son, if I had met him in California; for he looks so much like his papa.

Mrs. G. [*To the boy.*] Get out of here this minute. Go to the kitchen.   [*Exit* Sampey, r.
That is one of the niggers, sir.

Maj. M. I beg your pardon, madam; I beg your pardon.

Mrs. G. No offence, sir; mistakes will be made. Ah! here comes the Colonel.

Enter Dr. Gaines, m. d.

Dr. Gaines. Bless my soul, how are you, Major? I'm exceedingly pleased to see you. Be seated, be seated, Major.

Mrs. G. Please excuse me, gentlemen; I must go and look after dinner, for I've no doubt that the Major will have an appetite for dinner, by the time it is ready.

[*Exit* Mrs. Gaines, r.

Maj. M. Colonel, I'm afraid I've played the devil here to-day.

Dr. G. Why, what have you done?

Maj. M. You see, Colonel, I always make it a point, wherever I go, to praise the children, if there are any, and so to-day, seeing one of your little servants come in, and taking him to be your son, I spoke to your wife of the marked resemblance between you and the boy. I am afraid I've insulted madam.

Dr. G. Oh! do n't let that trouble you. Ha, ha, ha. If you did call him my son, you did n't miss it much. Ha, ha, ha. Come, we 'll take a walk, and talk over matters about old times.   [*Exit*, L.

Scene 4.—FOREST SCENERY.

Enter GLEN, L.

Glen. Oh, how I want to see Melinda! My heart pants and my soul is moved whenever I hear her voice. Human tongue cannot tell how my heart yearns toward her. Oh, God! thou who gavest me life, and implanted in my bosom the love of liberty, and gave me a heart to love, Oh, pity the poor outraged slave! Thou, who canst rend the veil of centuries, speak, Oh, speak, and put a stop to this persecution! What is death, compared to slavery? Oh, heavy curse, to have thoughts, reason, taste, judgment, conscience and passions like another man, and not have equal liberty to use them! Why was I born with a wish to be free, and still be a slave? Why should I call another man master? And my poor Melinda, she is taken away from me, and I dare not ask the tyrant where she is. It is childish to stand here weeping. Why should my eyes be filled with tears, when my brain is on fire? I will find my wife—I will; and wo to him who shall try to keep me from her!

Scene 5.—ROOM IN A SMALL COTTAGE ON THE POPLAR FARM,

(*Ten miles from Muddy Creek, and owned by Dr. Gaines.*)

Enter MELINDA, R.

Melinda. Here I am, watched, and kept a prisoner in this place. Oh, I would that I could escape, and once more get

with Glen. Poor Glen! He does not know where I am.
Master took the opportunity, when Glen was in the city with
his master, to bring me here to this lonely place, and fear-
ing that mistress would know where I was, he brought me
here at night. Oh, how I wish I could rush into the arms
of sleep!—that sweet sleep, which visits all alike, descend-
ing, like the dews of heaven, upon the bond as well as the
free. It would drive from my troubled brain the agonies of
this terrible night.

Enter Dr. Gaines, l.

Dr. Gaines. Good evening, Melinda! Are you not glad
to see me?

Melinda. Sir, how can I be glad to see one who has made
life a burden, and turned my sweetest moments into bitter-
ness?

Dr. G. Come, Melinda, no more reproaches! You know
that I love you, and I have told you, and I tell you again,
that if you will give up all idea of having Glen for a husband, I will set you free, let you live in this cottage, and be
your own mistress, and I'll dress you like a lady. Come,
now, be reasonable!

Melinda. Sir, I am your slave; you can do as you please
with the avails of my labor, but you shall never tempt me
to swerve from the path of virtue.

Dr. G. Now, Melinda, that black scoundrel Glen has been
putting these notions into your head. I'll let you know that
you are my property, and I'll do as I please with you. I'll
teach you that there is no limit to my power.

Melinda. Sir, let me warn you that if you compass my
ruin, a woman's bitterest curse will be laid upon your head,
with all the crushing, withering weight that my soul can
impart to it; a curse that shall cling to you throughout the
remainder of your wretched life; a curse that shall haunt
you like a spectre in your dreams by night, and attend upon
you by day; a curse, too, that shall embody itself in the
ghastly form of the woman whose chastity you will have
outraged. Command me to bury myself in yonder stream,
and I will obey you. Bid me do any thing else, but I be-
seech you not to commit a double crime,—outrage a woman, and make her false to her husband.

Dr. G. You got a husband! Who is your husband, and
when were you married?

Melinda. Glen is my husband, and I've been married four weeks. Old Uncle Joseph married us one night by moonlight. I see you are angry; I pray you not to injure my husband.

Dr. G. Melinda, you shall never see Glen again. I have bought him from Hamilton, and I will return to Muddy Creek, and roast him at the stake. A black villain, to get into my way in that manner! Here I've come ten miles to-night to see you, and this is the way you receive me!

Melinda. Oh, master, I beg you not to injure my husband! Kill me, but spare him! Do! do! he is my husband!

Dr. G You shall never see that black imp again, so good night, my lady! When I come again, you'll give me a more cordial reception. Good night!

[*Exit* DR. GAINES, L.

Melinda. I shall go distracted. I cannot remain here and know that Glen is being tortured on my account. I must escape from this place,—I must,—I must!

Enter CATO, R.

Cato. No, you ain't a-gwine to 'scape, nudder. Massa tells me to keep dese eyes on you, an' I is gwine to do it.

Melinda. Oh, Cato, do let me get away! I beg you, do!

Cato. No; I tells you massa telled me to keep you safe; an' ef I let you go, massa will whip me. [*Exit* CATO, L.

Enter MRS. GAINES, R.

Mrs. G. Ah, you trollop! here you are! Your master told me that he had sold you and sent you down the river, but I knew better; I knew it was a lie. And when he left home this evening, he said he was going to the city on business, and I knew that was a lie too, and determined to follow him, and see what he was up to. I rode all the way over here to-night. My side-saddle was lent out, and I had to ride ten miles bare-back, and I can scarcely walk; and your master has just left here. Now deny that, if you dare.

Melinda. Madam, I will deny nothing which is true. Your husband has just gone from here, but God knows that I am innocent of any thing wrong with him.

Mrs. G. It's a lie! I know better. If you are innocent, what are you doing here, cooped up in this cottage by yourself? Tell me that!

Melinda. God knows that I was brought here against my will, and I beg that you will take me away.

Mrs. G. Yes, Melinda, I will see that you are taken away, but it shall be after a fashion that you won't like. I know that your master loves you, and I intend to put a stop to it. Here, drink the contents of this vial,—drink it!

Melinda. Oh, you will not take my life,—you will not!

Mrs. G. Drink the poison this moment!

Melinda. I cannot drink it.

Mrs. G. I tell you to drink this poison at once. Drink it, or I will thrust this knife to your heart! The poison or the dagger, this instant! [*She draws a dagger; Melinda retreats to the back of the room, and seizes a broom.*

Melinda. I will not drink the poison! [*They fight;* Me-LINDA *sweeps off* Mrs. Gaines,—*cap, combs and curls. Curtain falls.*

ACT IV.

Scene 1.—Interior of a Dungeon—Glen in chains.

Glen. When I think of my unmerited sufferings, it almost drives me mad. I struck the doctor, and for that, I must remain here loaded with chains. But why did he strike me? He takes my wife from me, sends her off, and then comes and beats me over the head with his cane. I did right to strike him back again. I would I had killed him. Oh! there is a volcano pent up in the hearts of the slaves of these Southern States that will burst forth ere long. When that day comes, wo to those whom its unpitying fury may devour! I would be willing to die, if I could smite down with these chains every man who attempts to enslave his fellow-man.

Enter Sampey, r.

Sampey. Glen, I jess bin hear massa call de oberseer, and I spec somebody is gwine to be whipped. Anudder ting: I know whar massa took Linda to. He took her to de poplar farm, an' he went away las' night, an' missis she follow after massa, an' she ain't come back yet. I tell you, Glen, de debil will be to pay on dis place, but don't you tell any body dat I tole you.   [*Exit* SAMPEY, R.

Scene 2.—PARLOR.

DR. GAINES, *alone.*

Dr. Gaines. Yes, I will have the black rascal well whipped, and then I'll sell him. It was most fortunate for me that Hamilton was willing to sell him to me.

Enter MR. SCRAGG, L.

I have sent for you, Mr. Scragg. I want you to take Glen out of the dungeon, take him into the tobacco house, fasten him down upon the stretcher, and give him five hundred lashes upon his bare back; and when you have whipped him, feel his pulse, and report to me how it stands, and if he can bear more, I'll have you give him an additional hundred or two, as the case may be.

Scragg. I tell you, doctor, that suits me to a charm. I've long wanted to whip that nigger. When your brother-in-law came here to board, and brought that boy with him, I felt bad to see a nigger dressed up in such fine clothes, and I wanted to whip him right off. I tell you, doctor, I had rather whip that nigger than go to heaven, any day,— that I had!

Dr. G. Go, Mr. Scragg, and do your duty. Don't spare the whip!

Scragg. I will, sir; I'll do it in order. [*Exit* SCRAGG, L.

Dr. G. Every thing works well now, and when I get Glen out of the way, I'll pay Melinda another visit, and she'll give me a different reception. But I wonder where my wife is? She left word that she was going to see her brother, but I am afraid that she has got on my track. That woman is the pest of my life. If there's any place in heaven for her, I'd be glad if the Lord would take her home, for I've had her too long already. But what noise is that? What can that be? What is the matter?

Enter SCRAGG, L., *with face bloody.*

Scragg. Oh, dear me! oh, my head! That nigger broke away from me, and struck me over the head with a stick. Oh, dear me! Oh!

Dr. G. Where is he, Mr. Scragg?

Scragg. Oh! sir, he jumped out of the window; he's gone. Oh! my head; he's cracked my skull. Oh, dear me, I'm kilt! Oh! oh! oh!

Enter SLAVES, R.

Dr. G. Go, Dolly, and wash Mr. Scragg's head with some whiskey, and bind it up. Go at once. And Bob, you run over to Mr. Hall, and tell him to come with his hounds; we must go after the rascal.   [*Exit all except the* DOCTOR, R. This will never do. When I catch the scoundrel, I'll make an example of him; I'll whip him to death. Ah! here comes my wife. - I wonder what she comes now for? I must put on a sober face, for she looks angry.

Enter MRS. GAINES, L.

Ah! my dear, I am glad you've come, I've been so lonesome without you. Oh! Sarah, I do n't know what I should do if the Lord should take you home to heaven. I do n't think that I should be able to live without you.

Mrs. G. Dr. Gaines, you ought to be ashamed to sit there and talk in that way. You know very well that if the Lord should call me home to glory to-night, you'd jump for joy. But you need not think that I am going to leave this world before you. No; with the help of the Lord, I'll stay here to foil you in your meanness. I've been on your track, and a dirty track it is, too. You ought to be ashamed of yourself. See what promises you made me before we were married; and this is the way you keep your word. When I married you, every body said that it was a pity that a woman of my sweet temper should be linked to such a man as you.   [*She weeps and wrings her hands.*

Dr. G. Come, my dear, do n't make a fool of yourself. Come, let's go to supper, and a strong cup of tea will help your head.

Mrs. G. Tea help my head! tea won't help my head. You're a brute of a man; I always knew I was a fool for marrying you. There was Mr. Comstock, he wanted me, and he loved me, and he said I was an angel, so he did; and he loved me, and he was rich; and mother always said that he loved me more than you, for when he used to kiss me, he always squeezed my hand. You never did

2*

such a thing in your life. [*She weeps and wrings her hands.*

Dr. G. Come, my dear, do n't act so foolish.

Mrs. G. Yes; every thing I do is foolish. You 're a brute of a man; I won't live with you any longer. I 'll leave you — that I will. I 'll go and see a lawyer, and get a divorce from you — so I will.

Dr. G. Well, Sarah, if you want a divorce, you had better engage Mr. Barker. He 's the best lawyer in town; and if you want some money to facilitate the business, I 'll draw a check for you.

Mrs. G. So you want me to get a divorce, do you? Well, I won't have a divorce; no, I 'll never leave you, as long as the Lord spares me.   [*Exit* MRS. GAINES, R.

Scene 3. — FOREST AT NIGHT — LARGE TREE.

Enter MELINDA, L.

Melinda. This is indeed a dark night to be out and alone on this road. But I must find my husband, I must. Poor Glen! if he only knew that I was here, and could get to me, he would. What a curse slavery is! It separates husbands from their wives, and tears mothers from their helpless offspring, and blights all our hopes for this world. I must try to reach Muddy Creek before daylight, and seek out my husband. What 's that I hear? — footsteps? I 'll get behind this tree.

Enter GLEN, R.

Glen. It is so dark, I'm afraid I've missed the road. Still, this must be the right way to the poplar farm. And if Bob told me the truth, when he said that Melinda was at the poplar farm, I will soon be with her; and if I once get her in my arms, it will be a strong man that shall take her from me. Aye, a dozen strong men shall not be able to wrest her from my arms. [*Melinda rushes from behind the tree.*

Melinda. Oh, Glen! It is my husband,—it is!

Glen. Melinda! Melinda! it is, it is. Oh God! I thank Thee for this manifestation of Thy kindness. Come, come, Melinda, we must go at once to Canada. I escaped from the overseer, whom Dr. Gaines sent to flog me. Yes, I struck him over the head with his own club, and I made the wine flow freely; yes, I pounded his old skillet well for him, and then jumped out of the window. It was a leap for freedom. Yes, Melinda, it was a leap for freedom. I've said "master" for the last time. I am free; I'm bound for Canada. Come, let's be off, at once, for the negro dogs will be put upon our track. Let us once get beyond the Ohio river, and all will be right. [*Exit* R.

ACT V.

Scene 1. — Bar-Room in the American Hotel — Travellers lounging in Chairs, and at the Bar.

Enter Bill Jennings, R.

Barkeeper. Why, Jennings, how do you do?

Jennings. Say Mr. Jennings, if you please.

Barkeeper. Well, Mr. Jennings, if that suits you better. How are times? We've been expecting you, for some days.

Jennings. Well, before I talk about the times, I want my horses put up, and want you to tell me where my niggers are to stay to-night. Sheds, stables, barns, and every thing else here, seems pretty full, if I am a judge.

Barkeeper. Oh! I'll see to your plunder.

1st Lounger. I say, Barkeeper, make me a brandy cocktail, strong. Why, how do you do, Mr. Jennings?

Jennings. Pretty well, Mr. Peters. Cold evening, this.

1st. Loun. Yes, this is cold. I heard you speak of your niggers. Have you got a pretty large gang?

Jennings. No, only thirty-three. But they are the best that the country can afford. I shall clear a few dimes, this trip. I hear that the price is up.

Enter Mr. White, R.

White. Can I be accommodated here to-night, landlord?

Barkeeper. Yes, sir; we've bed for man and beast. Go, Dick, and take the gentleman's coat and hat. [*To the waiter.*] You're a stranger in these parts, I rec'on.

White. Yes, I am a stranger here.

2d Loun. Where mout you come from, ef it's a far question?

White. I am from Massachusetts.

3d Loun. I say, cuss Massachusetts!

1st Loun. I say so too. There is where the fanatics live; cussed traitors. The President ought to hang 'em all.

White. I say, landlord, if this is the language that I am to hear, I would like to go into a private room.

Barkeeper. We ain't got no private room empty.

1st Loun. Maybe you're mad 'bout what I said 'bout your State. Ef you is, I've only to say that this is a free country, and people talks what they please; an' ef you do n't like it, you can better yourself.

White. Sir, if this is a free country, why do you have slaves here? I saw a gang at the door, as I came in.

2d Loun. He did n't mean that this was a free country for niggers. He meant that it's free for white people. And another thing, ef you get to talking 'bout freedom for niggers, you 'll catch what you won't like, mister. It's right for niggers to be slaves.

White. But I saw some white slaves.

1st Loun. Well, they're white niggers.

White. Well, sir, I am from a free State, and I thank God for it; for the worst act that a man can commit upon his fellow-man, is to make him a slave. Conceive of a mind, a living soul, with the germs of faculties which infinity cannot exhaust, as it first beams upon you in its glad morning of existence, quivering with life and joy, exulting in the glorious sense of its developing energies, beautiful, and brave, and generous, and joyous, and free, — the clear pure spirit bathed in the auroral light of its unconscious immortality, — and then follow it in its dark and dreary passage through slavery, until oppression stifles and kills, one by one, every inspiration and aspiration of its being, until it becomes a dead soul entombed in a living frame!

3d Loun. Stop that; stop that, I say. That's treason to the country; that's downright rebellion.

Barkeeper. Yes, it is. And another thing, — this is not a meeting-house.

1st Loun. Yes, if you talk such stuff as that, you 'll get a chunk of cold lead in you, that you will.

Enter Dr. Gaines *and* Scragg, *followed by* Cato, r.

Dr. G. Gentlemen, I am in pursuit of two valuable slaves, and I will pay five hundred dollars for their arrest.

[*Exit* Mr. White, l.

1st Loun. I 'll bet a picayune that your niggers have been stolen by that cussed feller from Massachusetts. Don 't you see he 's gone ?

Dr. G. Where is the man ? If I can lay my hands on him, he 'll never steal another nigger. Where is the scoundrel ?

1st Loun. Let 's go after the feller. I 'll go with you. Come, foller me. [*Exit all*, l., *except* Cato *and the waiter.*

Cato. Why don 't you bring in massa's saddle-bags ? What de debil you standin' dar for ? You common country niggers do n't know nuffin', no how. Go an' get massa's saddle-bags, and bring 'em in.　　*Exit* Servant, r.
By golly ! ebry body 's gone, an' de bar-keeper too. I 'll tend de bar myself now ; an' de fuss gemman I waits on will be dis gemman of color. [*Goes behind the counter, and drinks.*] Ah, dis is de stuff fer me ; it makes my head swim ; it makes me happy right off. I 'll take a little more.

Enter Barkeeper, l.

Barkeeper. What are you doing behind that bar, you black cuss ?

Cato. I is lookin' for massa's saddle-bags, sir. Is dey here ?

Barkeeper. But what were you drinking there ?

Cato. Me drinkin' ! Why, massa, you muss be mistaken. I ain 't drink nuffin'.

Barkeeper. You infernal whelp, to stand there and lie in that way !

Cato. Oh, yes, seer, I did tase dat coffee in dat bottle ; dat 's all I did.

Enter Mr. White, l., *excited.*

Mr. White. I say, sir, is there no place of concealment in your house ? They are after me, and my life is in danger. Say, sir, can 't you hide me away ?

Barkeeper. Well, you ought to hold your tongue when you come into our State.

Mr. White. But, sir, the Constitution gives me the right to speak my sentiments, at all times and in all places.

Barkeeper. We don't care for Constitutions nor nothin' else. We made the Constitution, and we'll break it. But you had better hide away; they are coming, and they'll lynch you, that they will. Come with me; I'll hide you in the cellar. Foller me. [*Exit* BARKEEPER *and* WHITE, L.

Enter the MOB, R.

Dr. Gaines. If I can once lay my hands on that scoundrel, I'll blow a hole through his head.

Jennings. Yes, I say so too; for no one knows whose niggers are safe, now-a-days. I must look after my niggers. Who is that I see in the distance? I believe it's that cussed Massachusetts feller. Come, let's go after him. [*Exit the* MOB, R.

Scene 2.—FOREST AT NIGHT.

Enter GLEN *and* MELINDA, R.

Melinda. I am so tired and hungry, that I cannot go further. It is so cloudy that we cannot see the North Star, and therefore cannot tell whether we are going to Canada, or further South. Let's sit down here.

Glen. I know that we cannot see the North Star, Melinda, and I fear we've lost our way. But, see! the clouds are passing away, and it'll soon be clear. See! yonder is a star; yonder is another and another. Ah! yonder is the North Star, and we are safe!

> "Star of the North! though night winds drift
>   The fleecy drapery of the sky
> Between thy lamp and me, I lift,
>   Yea, lift with hope my sleepless eye,
> To the blue heights wherein thou dwellest,
> And of a land of freedom tellest.
>
> "Star of the North! while blazing day
>   Pours round me its full tide of light,
> And hides thy pale but faithful ray,
>   I, too, lie hid, and long for night:
> For night: I dare not walk at noon,
> Nor dare I trust the faithless moon—
>
> "Nor faithless man, whose burning lust
>   For gold hath riveted my chain,—
> Nor other leader can I trust
>   But thee, of even the starry train;

For all the host around thee burning,
Like faithless man, keep turning, turning.

"I may not follow where they go : —
    Star of the North ! I look to thee
While on I press ; for well I know,
    Thy light and truth shall set me free : —
Thy light, that no poor slave deceiveth ;
Thy truth, that all my soul believeth.

"Thy beam is on the glassy breast
    Of the still spring, upon whose brink
I lay my weary limbs to rest,
    And bow my parching lips to drink.
Guide of the friendless negro's way,
I bless thee for this quiet ray !

"In the dark top of southern pines
    I nestled, when the Driver's horn
Called to the field, in lengthening lines,
    My fellows, at the break of morn.
And there I lay till thy sweet face
Looked in upon " my hiding place."

"The tangled cane-brake, where I crept
    For shelter from the heat of noon,
And where, while others toiled, I slept,
    Till wakened by the rising moon,
As its stalks felt the night wind free,
Gave me to catch a glimpse of thee.

"Star of the North ! in bright array
    The constellations round thee sweep,
Each holding on its nightly way,
    Rising, or sinking in the deep,
And, as it hangs in mid heaven flaming,
The homage of some nation claiming.

" *This* nation to the Eagle cowers ;
    Fit ensign ! she's a bird of spoil : —
Like worships like ! for each devours
    The earnings of another's toil.
I've felt her talons and her beak,
And now the gentler Lion seek.

"The Lion, at the Monarch's feet
    Crouches, and lays his mighty paw
Into her lap ! — an emblem meet
    Of England's Queen, and English law :
Queen, that hath made her Islands free !
Law, that holds out its shield to me !

"Star of the North! upon that shield
   Thou shinest, — Oh, for ever shine!
The negro, from the cotton field
   Shall, then, beneath its orb recline,
And feed the Lion, couched before it,
Nor heed the Eagle, screaming o'er it!"

With the thoughts of servitude behind us, and the North Star before us, we will go forward with cheerful hearts. Come, Melinda, let's go on.   [*Exit*, L.

Scene 3.—A STREET.

Enter MR. WHITE, R.

Mr. White. I am glad to be once more in a free State. If I am caught again south of Mason and Dixon's line, I'll give them leave to lynch me. I came near losing my life. This is the way our constitutional rights are trampled upon. But what care these men about Constitutions, or any thing else that does not suit them? But I must hasten on.

      [*Exit*, L.

Enter CATO, *in disguise*, R.

Cato. I wonder ef dis is me? By golly, I is free as a frog. But maybe I is mistaken; maybe dis ain't me. Cato, is dis you? Yes, seer. Well, now it is me, an' I em a free man. But, stop! I muss change my name, kase ole massa might foller me, and somebody might tell him dat dey seed Cato; so I'll change my name, and den he won't know me ef he sees me. Now, what shall I call myself? I'm now in a suspectable part of de country, an' I muss have a suspectable name. Ah! I'll call myself Alexander Washington Napoleon Pompey Cæsar. Dar, now, dat's a good long, suspectable name, and every body will suspect me. Let me see; I wonder ef I can't make up a song on my escape? I'll try.

AIR— "*Dearest Mae.*"

Now, freemen, listen to my song, a story I'll relate,
It happened in de valley of de ole Kentucky State:
Dey marched me out into de fiel', at every break of day,
And work me dar till late sunset, widout a cent of pay.

   Chorus.—Dey work me all de day,
      Widout a bit of pay,
      And thought, because dey fed me well,
      I would not run away.

Massa gave me his ole coat, an' thought I'd happy be,
But I had my eye on de North Star, an' thought of liberty ;
Ole massa lock de door, an' den he went to sleep,
I dress myself in his bess clothes, an' jump into de street.

> *Chorus.*—Dey work me all de day,
> Widout a bit of pay,
> So I took my flight, in the middle of de night,
> When de sun was gone away.

Sed I, dis chile's a freeman now, he'll be a slave no more ;
I travell'd faster all dat night, dan I ever did before.
I came up to a farmer's house, jest at de break of day,
And saw a white man standin' dar, sed he, " You are a runaway."

> *Chorus.*—Dey work me all de day, &c.

I tole him I had left de whip, an' bayin' of de hound,
To find a place where man is man, ef sich dar can be found ;
Dat I had heard, in Canada, dat all mankind are free,
An' dat I was going dar in search of liberty.

> *Chorus.*—Dey work me all de day, &c.

I've not committed any crime, why should I run away ?
Oh ! shame upon your laws, dat drive me off to Canada.
You loudly boast of liberty, an' say your State is free,
But ef I tarry in your midst, will you protect me ?

> *Chorus.*—Dey work me all de day, &c.

[*Exit*, L.

Scene 4.—Dining-Room.—Table Spread.

Mrs. Neal *and* Charlotte.

Mrs. Neal. Thee may put the tea to draw, Charlotte. Thy father will be in soon, and we must have breakfast.

Enter Mr. Neal, L.

I think, Simeon, it is time those people were called. Thee knows that they may be pursued, and we ought not to detain them long here.

Mr. Neal. Yes, Ruth, thou art right. Go, Charlotte, and knock on their chamber door, and tell them that breakfast is ready.   [*Exit* Charlotte, R.

Mrs. N. Poor creatures ! I hope they'll reach Canada in safety. They seem to be worthy persons.

Enter Charlotte, R.

Charlotte. I've called them, mother, and they'll soon be down. I'll put the breakfast on the table.

Enter NEIGHBOR JONES, L.

Mr. N. Good morning, James. Thee has heard, I presume, that we have two very interesting persons in the house?

Jones. Yes, I heard that you had two fugitives by the Underground road, last night; and I've come over to fight for them, if any persons come to take them back.

Enter THOMAS, R.

Mr. N. Go, Thomas, and harness up the horses and put them to the covered wagon, and be ready to take these people on, as soon as they get their breakfast. Go, Thomas, and hurry thyself.   [*Exit* THOMAS, R.
And so thee wants to fight, this morning, James?

Jones. Yes; as you belongs to a society that don't believe in fighting, and I does believe in that sort of thing, I thought I'd come and relieve you of that work, if there is any to be done.

Enter GLEN *and* MELINDA, R.

Mr. N. Good morning, friends. I hope thee rested well, last night.

Mrs. N. Yes, I hope thee had a good night's rest.

Glen. I thank you, madam, we did.

Mr. N. I'll introduce thee to our neighbor, James Jones. He's a staunch friend of thy people.

Jones. I am glad to see you. I've come over to render assistance, if any is needed.

Mrs. N. Come, friends, take seats at the table. Thee'll take seats there. [*To* GLEN *and* MELINDA.] [*All take seats at the table.*] Does thee take sugar and milk in thy tea?

Melinda. I thank you, we do.

Jones. I'll look at your *Tribune*, Uncle Simeon, while you're eating.

Mr. N. Thee'll find it on the table.

Mrs. N. I presume thee's anxious to get to thy journey's end?

Glen. Yes, madam, we are. I am told that we are not safe in any of the free States.

Mr. N. I am sorry to tell thee, that that is too true. Thee will not be safe until thee gets on British soil. I won-

der what keeps Thomas; he should have been here with
the team.

Enter THOMAS, L.

Thomas. All's ready; and I've written the prettiest song
that was ever sung. I call it "The Underground Railroad."

Mr. N. Thomas, thee can eat thy breakfast far better
than thee can write a song, as thee calls it. Thee must
hurry thyself, when I send thee for the horses, Thomas.
Here lately, thee takes thy time.

Thomas. Well, you see I've been writing poetry; that's
the reason I've been so long. If you wish it, I'll sing it to
you.

Jones. Do let us hear the song.

Mrs. Neal. Yes, if Thomas has written a ditty, do let us
hear it.

Mr. Neal. Well, Thomas, if thee has a ditty, thee may
recite it to us.

Thomas. Well, I'll give it to you. Remember that I
call it, "The Underground Railroad."

AIR—*" Wait for the Wagon."*

Oh, where is the invention
　　Of this growing age,
Claiming the attention
　　Of statesman, priest, or sage,
In the many railways
　　Through the nation found,
Equal to the Yankees'
　　Railway under-ground?

　　Chorus.—No one hears the whistle,
　　　　Or rolling of the cars,
　　　　　While negroes ride to freedom
　　　　　Beyond the stripes and stars.

On the Southern borders
　　Are the Railway stations,
Negroes get free orders
　　While on the plantations;
For all, of ev'ry color,
　　First-class cars are found,
While they ride to freedom
　　By Railway under-ground.

　　Chorus.—No one hears the whistle, &c.

Masters in the morning
  Furiously rage,
Cursing the inventions
  Of this knowing age;
Order out the bloodhounds,
  Swear they'll bring them back,
Dogs return exhausted,
  Cannot find the track.

    Chorus.—No one hears the whistle, &c.

Travel is increasing,
  Build a double track,
Cars and engines wanted,
  They'll come, we have no lack.
Clear the track of loafers,
  See that crowded car!
Thousands passing yearly,
  Stock is more than par.

    Chorus.—No one hears the whistle, &c.

Jones. Well done! That's a good song. I'd like to have a copy of them verses. [*Knock at the door. Charlotte goes to the door, and returns.*

    Enter Cato, L., *still in disguise.*

Mr. Neal. Who is this we have? Another of the outcasts, I presume?

Cato. Yes, seer; I is gwine to Canada, an' I met a man, an' he tole me dat you would give me some wittals an' help me on de way. By golly! ef dar ain't Glen an' Melinda. Dey don't know me in dese fine clothes. [*Goes up to them.*] Ah, chillen! I is one wid you. I golly, I is here too! [*They shake hands.*]

Glen. Why, it is Cato, as I live!

Melinda. Oh, Cato, I am so glad to see you! But how did you get here?

Cato. Ah, chile, I come wid ole massa to hunt you; an' you see I get tired huntin' you, an' I am now huntin' for Canada. I leff de ole boss in de bed at de hotel; an' you see I thought, afore I left massa, I'd jess change clothes wid him; so, you see, I is fixed up,—ha, ha, ha. Ah, chillen! I is gwine wid you.

Mrs. Neal. Come, sit thee down, and have some breakfast.

Cato. Tank you, madam, I'll do dat. [*Sits down and eats.*

Mr. Neal. This is pleasant for thee to meet one of thy friends.

Glen. Yes, sir, it is; I would be glad if we could meet more of them. I have a mother and sister still in slavery, and I would give worlds, if I possessed them, if by so doing I could release them from their bondage.

Thomas. We are all ready, sir, and the wagon is waiting.

Mrs. Neal. Yes, thee had better start.

Cato. Ef any body tries to take me back to ole massa, I'll pull ebry toof out of dar-heads, dat I will! As soon as I get to Canada, I'll set up a doctor shop, an' won't I be poplar? Den I rec'on I will. I'll pull teef fer all de people in Canada. Oh, how I wish I had Hannah wid me! It makes me feel bad when I tink I ain't a-gwine to see my wife no more. But, come, chillen, let's be makin' tracks. Dey say we is most to de British side.

Mr. Neal. Yes, a few miles further, and you'll be safe beyond the reach of the Fugitive-Slave Law.

Cato. Ah, dat's de talk fer dis chile.   [*Exit*, M. D.

Scene 5.—The Niagara River—A Ferry.

Ferryman, *fastening his small boat.*

Ferryman, [*advancing, takes out his watch.*] I swan, if it ain't one o'clock. I thought it was dinner time. Now there's no one here, I'll go to dinner, and if any body comes, they can wait until I return. I'll go at once.

          [*Exit*, L.

Enter Mr. White, R., *with an umbrella.*

Mr. White. I wonder where that ferryman is? I want to cross to Canada. It seems a little showery, or else the mist from the Falls is growing thicker. [*Takes out his sketch-book and pencils,—sketches.*

Enter Cane Pedlar, R.

Pedlar. Want a good cane to-day, sir? Here's one from Goat Island,—very good, sir,—straight and neat,— only one dollar. I've a wife and nine small children,— youngest is nursing, and the oldest only three years old. Here's a cane from Table Rock, sir. Please buy one!

I 've had no breakfast to-day. My wife 's got the rheumatics, and the children 's got the measles. Come, sir, do buy a cane! I 've a lame shoulder, and can 't work.

Mr. White. Will you stop your confounded talk, and let me alone? Don 't you see that I am sketching? You 've spoiled a beautiful scene for me, with your nonsense.

Enter 2d Pedlar, R.

2d Pedlar. Want any bead bags, or money purses? These are all real Ingen bags, made by the Black Hawk Ingens. Here 's a pretty bag, sir, only 75 cents. Here 's a money purse, 50 cents. Please, sir, buy something! My wife 's got the fever and ague, and the house is full of children, and they 're all sick. Come, sir, do help a worthy man!

Mr. White. Will you hold your tongue? You 've spoiled some of the finest pictures in the world. Don 't you see that I am sketching?   [*Exit* Pedlars, R., *grumbling.*
I am glad those fellows have gone; now I 'll go a little further up the shore, and see if I can find another boat. I want to get over.   [*Exit*, L.

Enter Dr. Gaines, Scragg, *and an* Officer.

Officer. I do n't think that your slaves have crossed yet, and my officers will watch the shore below here, while we stroll up the river. If I once get my hands on them, all the Abolitionists in the State shall not take them from me.

Dr. G. I hope they have not got over, for I would not lose them for two thousand dollars, especially the gal.

Enter 1st Pedlar.

Pedlar. Wish to get a good cane, sir? This stick was cut on the very spot where Sam Patch jumped over the falls. Only fifty cents. I have a sick wife and thirteen children. Please buy a cane; I ain't had no dinner.

Officer. Get out of the way! Gentlemen, we 'll go up the shore.   [*Exit*, L.

Enter Cato, R.

Cato. I is loss fum de cumpny, but dis is de ferry, and I spec dey 'll soon come. But did n't we have a good time las' night in Buffalo? Dem dar Buffalo gals make my heart flutter, dat dey did. But, tanks be to de Lord, I is got

religion. I got it las' night in de meetin.' Before I got
religion, I was a great sinner; I got drunk, an' took de
name of de Lord in vain. But now I is a conwerted man;
I is bound for hebben; I toats de witness in my bosom; I
feel dat my name is rote in de book of life. But dem niggers in de Vine Street Church las' night shout an' make sich
a fuss, dey give me de headache. But, tank de Lord, I is
got religion, an' now I 'll be a preacher, and den dey 'll call
me de Rev. Alexander Washinton Napoleon Pompey Cæsar.
Now I 'll preach and pull teef, bofe at de same time. Oh,
how I wish I had Hannah wid me! Cuss ole massa, fer ef
it warn't for him, I could have my wife wid me. Ef I
had n't religion, I 'd say " Damn ole massa !" but as I is a
religious man, an' belongs to de church, I won't say no sich
a thing. But who is dat I see comin'? Oh, it 's a whole
heap of people. Good Lord! what is de matter?

Enter GLEN *and* MELINDA, L., *followed by* OFFICERS.

Glen. Let them come; I am ready for them. He that
lays hands on me or my wife shall feel the weight of this
club.

Melinda. Oh, Glen, let 's die here, rather than again go
into slavery.

Officer. I am the United States Marshal. I have a war-
rant from the Commissioner to take you, and bring you
before him. I command assistance.

Enter DR. GAINES, SCRAGG, *and* OFFICER, R.

Dr. Gaines. Here they are. Down with the villain!
down with him! but do n't hurt the gal!

Enter MR. WHITE, R.

Mr. White. Why, bless me! these are the slaveholding
fellows. I 'll fight for freedom! [*Takes hold of his umbrel-
la with both hands.—The fight commences, in which
GLEN, CATO, DR. GAINES, SCRAGG, WHITE, and the
OFFICERS, take part.—FERRYMAN enters, and runs to
his boat.—DR. GAINES, SCRAGG and the OFFICERS are
knocked down, GLEN, MELINDA and CATO jump into
the boat, and as it leaves the shore and floats away,
GLEN and CATO wave their hats, and shout loudly for
freedom.—Curtain falls.*

THE END.

COSIMO is a specialty publisher of books and publications that inspire, inform, and engage readers. Our mission is to offer unique books to niche audiences around the world.

COSIMO BOOKS publishes books and publications for innovative authors, nonprofit organizations, and businesses. **COSIMO BOOKS** specializes in bringing books back into print, publishing new books quickly and effectively, and making these publications available to readers around the world.

COSIMO CLASSICS offers a collection of distinctive titles by the great authors and thinkers throughout the ages. At **COSIMO CLASSICS** timeless works find new life as affordable books, covering a variety of subjects including: Business, Economics, History, Personal Development, Philosophy, Religion & Spirituality, and much more!

COSIMO REPORTS publishes public reports that affect your world, from global trends to the economy, and from health to geopolitics.

FOR MORE INFORMATION CONTACT US AT
INFO@COSIMOBOOKS.COM

- if you are a book lover interested in our current catalog of books

- if you represent a bookstore, book club, or anyone else interested in special discounts for bulk purchases

- if you are an author who wants to get published

- if you represent an organization or business seeking to publish books and other publications for your members, donors, or customers.

COSIMO BOOKS ARE ALWAYS
AVAILABLE AT ONLINE BOOKSTORES

VISIT COSIMOBOOKS.COM
BE INSPIRED, BE INFORMED